WITHDRAWN

CONTEMPORARY LIVES

DRAKE

ACTOR & HIP-HOP ARTIST

ABDO
Publishing Company

DRAKE

ACTOR & HIP-HOP ARTIST

by Steve Otfinoski

CREDITS

Published by ABDO Publishing Company, PO Box 398166,
Minneapolis, MN 55439. Copyright © 2013 by Abdo Consulting
Group, Inc. International copyrights reserved in all countries.
No part of this book may be reproduced in any form without
written permission from the publisher. The Essential Library™ is a
trademark and logo of ABDO Publishing Company.

Printed in the United States of America,
North Mankato, Minnesota
092012
012013

 THIS BOOK CONTAINS AT LEAST 10% RECYCLED MATERIALS.

Editor: Rebecca Felix
Series Designer: Emily Love

Cataloging-in-Publication Data
Otfinoski, Steve.
 Drake: actor & hip-hop artist / Steve Otfinoski.
   p. cm. -- (Contemporary lives)
Includes bibliographical references and index.
ISBN 978-1-61783-618-3
1. Drake, 1986- --Juvenile literature. 2. Actor--Canada--Biography-
-Juvenile literature. 3. Rap musicians--Canada--Biography--Juvenile
literature. 1. Title.
782.421649092--dc15
[B]
                                                    2012945962

TABLE OF CONTENTS

Drake attended his first
Grammy Awards in 2010.

CHAPTER 1

A Star is Born

||||||||||||||||||||||||||||||||||||||||||||||||||||||||||||||||||||||||||||||||||||

The list of performers for the Grammy Awards on January 31, 2010, was star studded. Nominees and performers included pop music stars Lady Gaga and Elton John, young country music phenomenon Taylor Swift, rhythm and blues (R&B) star Beyoncé, and more. Songwriter and rapper Drake would perform as well, but he was not yet a star—or even well known. In fact, Drake didn't even have an album yet.

Nonetheless, he was about to make his Grammy debut among the music industry's biggest stars.

As each act appeared that night, the audience greeted it with enthusiastic cheers and applause. The atmosphere in the Los Angeles Staples Center was electric. The time came for the closing act of the evening. Rapper Lil Wayne, wearing a white jacket and white T-shirt that read, "Listen to Lil Wayne," took to the stage. He began singing the opening verse of his hit duet with rapper Eminem, "Drop the World." The audience went wild. Then Eminem strutted onstage, wearing a jacket and a knit cap, and sang another verse and chorus of their song. Both singers left in enough profanities

ADVICE FROM A PRO

While rehearsing for his debut performance at the Grammys, Drake was understandably nervous. He later told reporters how Eminem helped ease his nerves:

"Em gave me probably one of the best speeches . . . not really a speech, but . . . he gave me that reassurance. He was like, 'Man, anytime you need to look over at me, don't get nervous. Just look over at me, man, and I'll give it back to you. Everything will be all right. Don't be nervous.' For him to say that to me—I feel that was an important moment. It was nice."[1]

Lil Wayne, *left*, and Drake, *right*, performing at the Grammy Awards in 2010

to keep the network censors busy bleeping them out for the television audience. One reporter called it "the most heavily bleeped performance in Grammy history."[2]

When Eminem finished, rock band Blink-182's Travis Barker broke into another song on the drums. At that moment, a third singer, tall and handsome and dressed in a black leather jacket, stepped onstage. It was Drake, and when he joined Barker's drumming to sing "Forever," a song he penned, he earned his own warm applause from the crowd. As the performance ended, Drake hugged Lil Wayne and Eminem. The audience roared its approval.

Drake's debut was a notable addition to a night of outstanding performances. Adding to the amazing experience was the fact that newcomer Drake was also a nominee. He was up for awards in two categories that night, Best Rap Song and Best Rap Solo Performance, for his song "Best I Ever Had."

PUTTING OUT A RECORD

When an artist puts out a record, it is usually a collaboration of many people. In addition to promoting and negotiating live performances, an agent works to ensure record labels give an artist exposure when releasing an album. The record label helps the artist create, manufacture, and then distribute the album. A producer oversees and provides money for this process. In turn, the producer, agent, and record label all receive a portion of the artist's profits, outlined in a contract that is signed by all parties.

The program director for New York City's Hot 97 FM was surprised when the radio station started getting numerous calls requesting then-unknown Drake's song "Best I Ever Had." But he changed his tune after he heard the song. "It sounds like a hit song," he said. "It's catchy. It was being played in clubs and getting a big reaction. People were texting us, 'Hey, you're cool for playing this. Thank you!' . . . I put two and two together. We should be playing this guy's song!"[3]

Drake owed this feat to the popularity of "Best I Ever Had," which had been released the previous February. The song was on Drake's third independent mixtape, which means he created it himself, without help from a producer, agent, or record label. The mixtape was titled *So Far Gone* and released as a free download on Drake's official Web site on February 13, 2009. Listeners loved it so much they requested it on top radio stations, including New York City's Hot 97 FM. The constant airplay that followed led to the song being released commercially on iTunes in mid-June 2009. It sold an incredible 600,000 digital downloads and zoomed to Number 1 on *Billboard*'s Hot Rap Tracks. It peaked at Number 3 on *Billboard*'s Hot 100 by the summer of 2009. With just three mixtapes to his name and no album, Drake had become one of the hottest hip-hop artists in less than a year.

Drake's talent had brought him to the Grammy Awards, but so had some amazing luck. Lil Wayne, the singer he shared the Staples Center's stage with, had pulled Drake out of obscurity in 2008, after hearing one of his earlier mixtapes. Lil Wayne took the young Drake on tour with him and became his friend and mentor. He found Drake a manager and eventually signed him to record for Wayne's recording label Young Money Entertainment, an imprint of Universal Motown.

Although Drake did not end up winning either award he was nominated for at the Grammys in 2010, just being nominated and performing were amazing accomplishments.

"Whether I take them home or not, this is an amazing moment for me. Everybody knows the Grammys are the awards to receive as a musician. It symbolizes not popularity, but great music," he said.[4] Drake had arrived.

‖‖‖‖‖‖

The Grammys in 2010 were a high note for Drake, but it was just the start of a successful year packed with performances and nominations.

Aubrey's hometown of Toronto
in Ontario, Canada

CHAPTER 2

A Canadian Childhood

||||||||||||||||||||||||||||||||||||||||||||||||||||||

Aubrey Drake Graham was born in Toronto, Ontario, a province in Canada, on October 24, 1986. His father, Dennis, is an African-American musician who once played drums for rock star Jerry Lee Lewis. His Jewish-Canadian mother, Sandi, is a former teacher. When Aubrey was five, his parents divorced. His father moved back to his hometown of Memphis, Tennessee. Aubrey remained

Drake has always been very close to his mother. She was his date for the Grammy Awards in 2010. After becoming a rap star, he canceled a big tour to be by her side while she was in the hospital undergoing surgery. "My mother made me truly appreciate women," he has said. "And my father was basically a reverse role model for me. I'm dying to be a great dad one day, whenever that day comes. Other than that, it was hard just growing up with my mom and watching her fight for me to have a good childhood."[2]

in Toronto with his mother. "I had to become a man very quickly and be the backbone for a woman who I love with all my heart, my mother," Aubrey recalled years later.[1] He felt bitter about his father's abandonment of the family, a feeling that would somewhat soften as he got older and spent more time with his father.

||||||||||||||||||||||||||||||||||||||||||||||||||||||||||||||||

GROWING UP WITH JEWISH AND BLACK CULTURE

Aubrey lived with his mother in an apartment in Forest Hill, a middle-class, mostly Jewish neighborhood on the north side of Toronto. He attended Forest Hill Public School during

Drake with his mom, Sandi Graham, in 2011

elementary school. Aubrey's mother raised him in the Jewish faith and taught him to be proud of his heritage. Aubrey and Sandi celebrated all the Jewish holy days. When he was 13, Aubrey had a bar mitzvah, a religious rite where a boy becomes a man in the Jewish community.

Although he is proud of his Jewish heritage, Aubrey considers himself first and foremost a black man. "At the end of the day," Aubrey said, "I consider myself a black man because I'm more immersed in black culture than any other. Being Jewish is kind of a cool twist. It makes me unique."[3] This consciousness evolved slowly after Aubrey spent more time with his father. When the school year ended in Toronto, he would often travel to Memphis to spend the summer with his

SANDI'S ILLNESS

When Aubrey was still young, his mother developed the disease rheumatoid arthritis. The condition attacks a person's joints and inflames them. Due to this disease, Sandi became unable to work, and she was unsteady on her feet and susceptible to falls. "We would have this little drill where, Lord forbid something happened, if there was a fire or an emergency, he would have to run outside and get a neighbor and call 911," recalled Sandi.[4]

The music scene in Memphis, Tennessee, influenced Aubrey's future musical style and sound.

dad, where he was exposed to different types of music. Aubrey met his father's family and friends in Memphis and fell in love with the music they listened to: blues, R&B, and especially Southern rap. By the age of ten, Aubrey started writing his own songs.

In later years, Aubrey's relationship with his dad remained friendly, but it still contained an underlying bitterness from his abandonment of Aubrey when he was young. As Aubrey put it in an interview with *GQ* magazine,

> *Me and my dad are friends. We're cool. I'll never be disappointed again, because I don't expect anything anymore from him. I just let him exist, and that's how we get along.*[5]

MUSICAL FAMILY

Dennis is not the only musician in Aubrey's family. Two of Aubrey's uncles also made their living by playing music. Larry Graham played the bass guitar for rock stars including Prince and Sly and the Family Stone. He later founded his own soul group, Graham Central Station. Another uncle, Mabon Lewis "Teenie" Hodges, played lead and rhythm guitar and was also a gifted songwriter. He wrote or cowrote several hit songs for soul singer Al Green, including "Love and Happiness" and "Take Me to the River."

ACTING BUG

In eighth grade, Aubrey became interested in acting. One of his schoolmates had a father who was an agent. The agent told his son, "If there's anyone in the class that makes you laugh, have them audition for me."[6]

Aubrey's friend found him funny and offered him the chance to audition for his father. He took it. The agent was impressed with Aubrey's abilities as an actor and took him on as a client. As a result, 13-year-old Aubrey's life was about to undergo a dramatic change.

||||||||||

Aubrey found success as a teenage television actor.

CHAPTER 3

Television Star

IIIIIIIIIIIIIIIIIIIIIIIIIIIIIIIIIIIIIIIIIIIIIIIIIIIIIIIIIIIIIIIIIIIIIIIIIIIIIIIIIIIIIIIIIIII

I n 1979, Canadian television producers Linda Schuyler and Kit Hood had created a half-hour teen drama called *The Kids of Degrassi Street*. The show was about young people and their problems. The characters were students of Degrassi Community School, a fictitious high school in Toronto, although Degrassi Street is a real street in the city. The program eventually became one of the biggest hits in Canadian television. When it ended its run in

Just as the previous Degrassi series had done, *Degrassi: The Next Generation* became a worldwide hit and made stars of its cast members. In April 2002, the cast earned a Young Artist Award for Best Ensemble in a TV Series (Comedy or Drama). The show was entertaining but also serious, dealing with teen issues that were rarely explored on series television before, including peer pressure, bullying, teen pregnancy, depression, and drug and alcohol abuse.

1986, the creators produced a second series, *Degrassi Junior High*, which was later renamed *Degrassi High*. That series ran from 1987 to 1991. In the late 1990s, the producers decided to revive the show yet again. It would air in 2001. They would hire a new, young cast and call the series *Degrassi: The Next Generation*.

Aubrey's agent sent him to audition for the new show. The producers liked the 13-year-old's acting and gave him the role of Jimmy Brooks, a student from a wealthy family who is a star basketball player at Degrassi Community School.

||||||||||||||||||||||||||||||||||||||||||||||||||

The part of Jimmy Brooks was originally meant to be a white football player. But when the producers saw Aubrey's audition, they were willing to rewrite the part to fit the actor. Producer Schuyler recalled, "We were looking for an athletic, friend-of-everybody type. Aubrey had a charm about him, and a warmth, that same beautiful smile he has now. He was green as anything, but willing to do whatever it takes."[2]

A NEW LIFE

Landing the part on *Degrassi* changed Aubrey's life. He started attending a new school closer to the studio. It had a diverse student body, and Aubrey felt at home there. When he wasn't in school or at home, he was at the studio, rehearsing and filming the television show. He spent so much time there that some days he would sleep on the set rather than go home.

The series was soon airing in the United States, where it was shown on the Teen Nick Network. The cast did mall tours in the United States to promote the show. "We would get 3,000 or 4,000 kids and Aubrey even then had this aura about him as a rock star," remembers producer Schuyler.[1]

Aubrey, *second from left*, with fellow *Degrassi* cast members, including Shane Kippel, *far left*, who became Aubrey's close friend

Playing Jimmy Brooks on *Degrassi: The Next Generation* made Aubrey a television star. In an interview for a Canadian kids' magazine, he was asked how fame changed his life. He responded:

I don't know. But when I was young, I was like "Am I EVER going to get a date?" And now things

In *Degrassi*'s fourth season, Aubrey's character Jimmy Brooks went through some major changes. Jimmy had joined his buddy Spinner in bullying Rick, a brainy loner. When Jimmy and Rick were forced to appear together on a local television quiz show, they unexpectedly became friends. Unfortunately, Spinner and the other bullies led Rick to believe, incorrectly, that Jimmy had betrayed him. In a rage, Rick shot Jimmy at school. Jimmy survived as a paraplegic, his legs paralyzed. He became bound to a wheelchair and could no longer play basketball. To study for the changing role, Aubrey spent time with a teen who was shot in real life and left paralyzed.

have totally changed for me. I get mobbed at mall tours, and school and stuff. It's pretty crazy.[3]

||||||||||||||||||||||||||||||||||||||||||||||||||||||||||

BIRTH OF A RAPPER

His fame as an actor gave Aubrey the confidence to pursue his first love: music. He continued writing songs while acting and became more interested in rap. This increased interest stemmed from his father's situation. Aubrey's father was in prison, for reasons that are unclear—Aubrey later recalled it was possible drug or assault charges—when

Aubrey was approximately 14. His cellmate was a young, aspiring rapper. When Aubrey called his dad on the phone, Dennis would share some of his phone time with his cellmate, who rarely got phone calls. As Aubrey later recalled,

> [My dad] had a cellmate who used to rap, but he had nobody to talk to. I was probably 14; the guy was probably 21. My dad was like, "My son likes to rap so I'ma let you rap for him. I'ma share my phone time with you." . . . The guy's name was Poverty. . . . Next day, my dad would call me. So I'd pick up and he'd pass the phone and the guy rapped again. I had been writing raps but never rapped for anybody. I was like, "I'ma get my little rhyme book together tomorrow." And we'd go back and forth.[4]

By rapping back and forth over the phone, Poverty made Aubrey feel comfortable about performing. Aubrey began performing rap music in public at school functions.

As a rapper, Aubrey chose to go by his middle name, Drake. He began handing out homemade CDs of his songs to his fellow actors and the crew on the set of *Degrassi*. They were impressed by his music and urged him to share the CD with producer Schuyler. They thought she might decide to showcase his musical talents on the program. But Aubrey was reluctant at first, worried about his producer's reaction. Schuyler recalls, "He said, 'I do some swearing on [the CD] and I don't know if I want Linda to hear it.' Which is so cute."[5]

ROOM FOR IMPROVEMENT

In December 2005, Aubrey was thinking about recording a collection of the songs he had written. In February 2006, he recorded the songs on a mixtape with money he borrowed from an uncle. He started selling the mixtape, entitled *Room for Improvement*, and sold 6,000 copies. To reach

FIRST MIXTAPE

Room for Improvement was produced by professional mixer DJ Smallz, who had previously made mixtapes for such big-name rappers as Lil Wayne and Young Jeezy. It had a total of 22 tracks, 17 of them originals Aubrey wrote.

Other artists, including Toronto singer Voyce and Virginia artists Nickelus F. and Trey Songz, collaborated on some tracks. Aubrey was pleased with the mixtape and encouraged by the positive feedback it received from listeners.

a wider audience, he then released the mixtape for free on a Web site he had created and on his MySpace page, a social media Web site.

In an interview for a Canadian magazine, Aubrey was asked what he saw in his future. "I'm not really into predicting the future," he replied. "But whatever I do, I want it to be classy, timeless. If I can be known as someone who's conscious, and make a difference in the world, then that's what matters."[6] Before that would happen, however, there would be some bumps in the road to his musical fame.

||||||||||

Aubrey attended the Soul
Train Awards in 2006.

Drake appeared with *Degrassi* cast mates on MTV's *Total Request Live* in 2007, around the time he began gaining attention in the music world.

CHAPTER 4

Moving into Music

||||||||||||||||||||||||||||||||

he release of his first mixtape didn't make Drake a rap idol, but it did get him noticed in the music world. His songs were refreshingly different from most male rap songs at the time, which were full of boastful bragging. Drake's music, in contrast, was more emotional, sensitive, and lyrical. People were listening and responding to it.

Drake's character Jimmy Brooks went through several changes after being shot and confined to a wheelchair on *Degrassi*. Unable to play on the school basketball team, the character looked into many other hobbies. Similar to the actor that played him, the character took an interest in music, and he sang in the school talent show.

But while he didn't sing about the rapper lifestyle, Drake was somewhat interested in living it. He spent his *Degrassi* salary freely. He leased a brand-new Rolls-Royce Phantom, an expensive luxury car, which he parked in front of his mother's modest apartment. He also went into debt, much to Sandi's embarrassment.

|||||||||||||||||||||||||||||||||||||||||||||||||||

COMEBACK SEASON

On November 25, 2007, Drake released a second mixtape, called *Comeback Season*, with 24 tracks. Drake released one track, "Replacement Girl," as a single. It featured his friend, singer and rapper Trey Songz. "Replacement Girl" entered the *Billboard* Bubbling Under R&B/Hip-Hop Songs chart and peaked at Number 21. To capitalize on the song's

Trey Songz and Drake at the taping for BET's *106 and Park* on April 5, 2007

success, Drake produced a music video to go with the song.

The music video was picked up as the "New Joint of the Day" on Black Entertainment Television's (BET) hip-hop show *106 and Park* on April 30, 2007. It became the first music video to be featured on the network that was by a Canadian rapper without a recording contract.

Drake's musical success and ambitions eventually started affecting his acting career. By his last season, he often arrived late to the set of *Degrassi*. "By the last season, he was always late," said his current manager Cortez Bryant. "He'd be in the [music] studio till six, [when] call [time to start filming] was at six-thirty."[3]

Drake saw he was getting himself in hot water with the show, but he couldn't stop concentrating on his music first. "I was in so much trouble with the producers," he recalled. "I had like three and a half strikes against my name."[4]

RAPPING ON *DEGRASSI*

The *Degrassi* creators decided to showcase Drake's music on the program in 2007. "The writers say his lyrics are eloquent, clear, haunting, and he's going through a lot of genuine self-examination," said producer Schuyler.[1] *Degrassi* costar and director Stefan Brogren had praise as well: "I find his lyrics really truthful, about who he is . . . he raps about his experience."[2]

But Drake had some initial reservations about singing on the show. He was hesitant to mix his acting and rap careers, wanting to keep the two worlds and identities separate. But his friends on the show were persuasive. "We said whatever rap you do it doesn't have to be Drake-level hip-hop. In fact it needs to be less," said Brogren. "He did it in the end and I think he was happy."[5] Drake agreed it turned out well.

||||||||||||||||||||||||||||||||||||||||||||||||||||||

A SURPRISE ENDING

In 2008, Drake came to work one day on *Degrassi* and was told his character was being eliminated from the show, for reasons that were unclear. His character appeared throughout the full season in 2008, but only one episode that was aired in 2009. Several other actors were fired as well. "We were all kind of fired in our own way," remembers Drake. "It was devastating for a lot of us. Our names were

DEGRASSI: THE REST OF THE STORY ||||||||||||

Degrassi: The Next Generation carried on into its ninth season with new cast members and new storylines. In season nine, the producers moved the show to Canadian Television's MuchMusic Channel, which was aimed specifically at the youth market. The following year, the producers turned the 30-minute weekly drama into a daily soap opera. The show was still running and in its twelfth season in 2012.

Though he felt unhappy about his end on *Degrassi*, Drake kept focused on building his music career.

changed on our dressing rooms and we were like 'What's happening?'"[6]

After 154 episodes and eight years on a hit television series, Drake was out of a job. This change affected his music as well. He wanted to make a third mixtape, but now he had no regular income to pay for it. To continue building his music career, Drake knew he would have to find another way to earn a living until his music began making money. "I was coming to terms with the fact that, okay, people know me from *Degrassi*, but I might have to work at a restaurant or something just to keep things going," he explained.[7] But just as his future looked uncertain, Drake unexpectedly got a helping hand from a famous rapper.

||||||||||

Drake, *left*, and Lil Wayne, *right*,
performed together in 2009,
the year after they met.

CHAPTER 5
Lil Wayne Tour

||||||||||||||||||||||||||||||||||||||||||||||||||||||||||||||||||||||||||||||||

I n 2008, rapper Lil Wayne was one of the brightest stars in the world of rap music. One day, Jas Prince played Lil Wayne some songs from Drake's first two mixtapes. Jas Prince is the son of J. Prince, who is Lil Wayne's friend and the founder of Houston, Texas, hip-hop record company Rap-A-Lot. There are conflicting accounts of when exactly this occurred, but it was in either November or December of that year. Either way, Lil Wayne was so impressed by what he

Lil Wayne, whose real name is Dwayne Michael Carter Jr., was born in September 1982 in New Orleans, Louisiana, where he grew up in poverty. He has cultivated a tough street image. He wears tattoos all over his body and has spent time in prison. Similar to Drake, Lil Wayne's career in show business began at an early age. At age eight, he impressed the founders of Cash Money Records, and by age 11, he was signed as the youngest recording artist on the label's roster. He first sang in a duo and then became a member of the rap group Hot Boys. Lil Wayne's first solo album, *Tha Block is Hot*, came out in 1999 and sold more than 1 million copies in the United States. After two lesser-selling albums, he produced a trilogy of hit albums, *Tha Carter* (2004), *Tha Carter II* (2006-2007), and *Tha Carter III* (2008). *Tha Carter III* was his most successful album through 2012, selling more than 1 million copies in its first week in the United States and winning a Grammy for Best Rap Album in 2009.

heard that he called Drake on the phone that same night and invited him to fly to Houston to join his ongoing tour. Drake was stunned. He accepted the invitation, and his professional music career was launched.

|||||||||||||||||||||||||||||||||||||||||||||||||||||||||||

LIFE ON TOUR

Being whisked to Houston to meet a high-profile rapper was quite an experience for young Drake. As he later recalled,

> I showed up to Houston and I was staying at the Hotel Derek, I remember. They brought me to my room and I was just in disbelief, like, "What am I doing here?" You know? For me it was surreal.[1]

Drake's first meeting in Houston with Lil Wayne was unusual. "He was . . . getting these big wings tattooed on his body on the tour bus for like six straight hours," recalled Drake.[2] Suddenly, Lil Wayne's entourage descended. "And out of nowhere, everyone got on the bus and the bus started moving. I just kept my mouth shut."[3] Although exciting and surreal, the raucous everyday occurrences of life on tour with Lil Wayne were intimidating. In another interview, Drake explained, "I sat in the same place on the bus for a week. I was scared."[4]

A week after Drake joined the tour, they arrived in Atlanta, Georgia. There, Drake got to perform for the first time with Lil Wayne. Singing with Wayne, he began to gain confidence and feel more at home with the other musicians on the tour. Drake quickly became an important part of Lil Wayne's Young Money Crew, an entourage of talented young singers and musicians, named after his record label, Young Money Entertainment.

The more Lil Wayne heard Drake perform, the more impressed he became with his talent. "I don't know anyone else out there that can touch [his music], including my stuff," Lil Wayne told *MTV News* years later. "That kid is on another planet."[5] By early 2009, Drake was opening for Lil Wayne on his concert tour, and the two were collaborating on several songs together.

||||||||||||||||||||||||||||||||||||||||||||||||||||||||||

SO FAR GONE

Prior to meeting Lil Wayne, Drake had started writing songs for another mixtape. He continued working on the collection of songs while under Lil Wayne's wing, and he has said the album tells of that time in his life like a story. The mixtape starts with the end of Drake's time on *Degrassi* and the end of a relationship. Drake wrote more new music in hotel rooms and on the road. Some of the songs were melancholy and sad. Additional tracks speak

Drake, *center rear*, became a part of Lil Wayne's Young Money Crew and soon collaborated on many songs with the artist.

to the many changes happening in Drake's life at the time. He explained the mixtape's journey:

It starts in January 2008 when I was kinda confused. . . . I gave up acting all together to really do this music thing, and I was really truly confused. . . . Not only was I confused about my career, I was also in a very destructive sort of . . . exhausting relationship with a female and it was just a bad headspace for me to be in. So that's where the tape starts. . . . I just felt that nothing was ever good enough, and she was always searching for more excitement and then we move into "Successful.". . . Then it goes into "Let's Call It Off," which is the breakup. And then coincidentally when I broke up with that girl a week later I went to Houston and met Lil Wayne and that's where "November 18" comes from.[6]

Although Drake titled the song "November 18," Lil Wayne's tour played Houston on December 18, making the dates contradictory. "November 18"

DRAKE'S IDEAL GIRL

In his early twenties when his fame began to rise, the good-looking Drake attracted much attention from female fans. Unlike many rappers who cultivated a tough image with women, Drake saw himself as gentler. In one interview, he spoke of his ideal girl. "She is very funny, very supportive, understands that right now I'm trying to build with somebody," he said. "The ideal girl is driven, working on something other than modeling or being a singer."[7]

and the other songs would make up Drake's third mixtape, titled *So Far Gone*. Lil Wayne helped with the production and sang on some tracks with Drake. One song Lil Wayne and Drake collaborated on, "Ransom," was later reconceived as "I Want This Forever" and still later developed into "Forever," the song they would sing together live with Eminem at the 2010 Grammy Awards. Drake's friend Songz and other artists including rapper Bun B., R&B singer Omarion, and producer Noah "40" Shebib also worked on a few songs for *So Far Gone*.

About the same time, Lil Wayne asked his manager, Cortez Bryant, to take Drake on as a client. Bryant did not need to be persuaded. He said of Drake, "Here's a guy who's not an established artist, and lyrically he's close to or on the same level as Lil Wayne."[8] With a manager and a team of collaborating artists behind him and a mixtape that was a more professional product than his first two efforts, Drake would end up in the spotlight at last.

‖‖‖‖‖‖‖

In 2009, Drake's fame rose and his music gained recognition.

CHAPTER 6

The Next Big Thing

||||||||||||||||||||||||||||||||||||||||||||||||||||||

Drake released the mixtape *So Far Gone* on February 13, 2009, as a free download on his personal Web site. The mixtape's emotional, soul-searching songs struck a chord with listeners. More than 8,000 people downloaded it within the first two hours of its release. The mixtape quickly became a media sensation, and a release party was held in Toronto. Basketball star LeBron James, a friend of Drake's, hosted the party. One track, "Best I Ever Had," in which Drake praised a woman he'd been in a good relationship with, was everyone's favorite. By April 2010, due to listeners' demand, the song began getting airplay around the country. Hot 97 FM in New York City played "Best I Ever Had" 1,300 times. Getting such radio exposure was unheard of for a song on a mixtape and by an unknown artist.

Although Drake did not have a record label behind him when he released *So Far Gone*, he did have Lil Wayne's wisdom and guidance plus that of a management team that included Bryant and Gee Roberson and Al Branch of the top firm Hip Hop Since 1978. Branch created a new word to describe the relationship between Lil Wayne and Drake: "cooperition." As he further explained,

> *It's when competition cooperates together. [Lil] Wayne is cooperating with Drake to achieve a common goal, to help each other out. The competition aspect is each rapper wants to be the best rapper that ever lived. But Wayne realized that in order to be great, you also have to collaborate with the best.[1]*

Drake performing at S.O.B.'s on May 26, 2009

RISING FAME

On May 26, Drake made his unofficial New York
debut at the club S.O.B.'s for a sold-out show.
The club's capacity is 450 people. Among those
people present were some of the most influential
people in the music and media business, including
record executives, performers, reporters, radio
personalities, and bloggers. As a *New York
Times* article stated, "How the show would be
processed was as important as how it would be
performed."[2] It was Drake's chance to make a big

impression on the media, and he felt the pressure. He later recalled, "When I was at S.O.B.'s, it was a lot of nerves. I was nervous. Not only that, but it just had so much pressure behind the show. Not only that, but I had no band. I had no sense of what makes a great performance."[3]

There were highs and lows during the performance, which the *New York Times* chronicled the next day. In its review of Drake, the article stated, "At moments he seemed uncertain, far more so than in videos of recent shows elsewhere. . . . There were flashes of the cleverness that has made Drake a force, though. . . . It may seem early in Drake's career for such laments, but such is the price of accelerated fame.[4]"

Ultimately, the show had a positive impact on Drake's career. After that show, many music industry insiders were calling Drake hip-hop's next big thing. In addition to recording tracks with Lil Wayne, Drake also began recording with a host of other well-known rappers, hip-hop, and R&B artists including Jay-Z, Rihanna, Jamie Foxx, Kanye West, and Mary J. Blige.

Popular hip-hop and soul singer Mary J. Blige was so impressed when she heard "Best I've Ever Had," that she called Drake the "savior."[6] As she explained for a film crew at Summer Jam '09, "The kid Drake is the best. I love what they're singing about, they're bigging up women again. They're making women feel special."[7]

Drake's newfound fame did have its downsides. Being a star in Canada, which had few stars in the music world, also made him a target. As he put it, "I'm a one of one. There's no one else you can hate as much as me if you hate money, or you hate success."[5] In May, Drake was robbed at gunpoint in a Toronto restaurant. When he cooperated with the police in their investigation of the crime, he was harshly criticized by some in the rap world for being an informant.

Many of these same people thought Drake's music was weak and said he didn't have the street credentials to be a top rapper. Unlike Lil Wayne and others, Drake didn't grow up in poverty, hadn't been involved in criminal activities, and didn't have tattoos all over his body. But what some saw as weaknesses, Drake saw as strengths. "I try to really capitalize off of what other rappers really can't do," he has said. "I have a different image."[8]

Rather than bashing him, some people in the music industry began trying to get a share of Drake's success. On May 28, 2009, the Canadian record company Canadian Money Entertainment released an album, *The Girls Love Drake*, on iTunes and other online outlets, featuring several songs from *So Far Gone*. Drake's manager called the release "a straight bootleg, a scandal" and sent a letter to the company to stop selling it.[9] The album was pulled from all outlets, but Canadian Money Entertainment founder Peter Greenwood claimed he had done it to help Drake, not hurt him. "We wanted to get more exposure for it [Drake's music] on the net," he said. "Breaking him in the states along with other Toronto artists has always been our goal. Drake is our hometown hero."[10]

By June 2009, "Best I Ever Had" broke into the top ten on the *Billboard* R&B/Hip-Hop Songs chart. Also that month, Drake released the song on iTunes, and it sold 600,000 digital downloads. That number was startling, considering the song had previously been available for free on the Internet.

After he released "Best I Ever Had," Drake soon found himself the object of a lawsuit, made against him by US rapper and producer Kia Shine. Shine claimed he had produced and cowrote "Best I Ever Had" and wanted 25 percent of its royalties.

Drake had never met Shine. Shine's claim rested on the fact that he had produced a previous mixtape track for Lil Wayne called "Do It for the Boy." He claimed: "Drake sampled the melody, some of the words, cadence, etc." from the song.[12] Drake admitted he had borrowed the line from Lil Wayne's song, but declared, "I wrote the entire composition in Toronto and I borrowed one line from a Lil Wayne song that he [Shine] produced the BEAT for. The claims of 25 percent ownership are false and for an artist to brag about splits on a song is distasteful to begin with."[13] As of 2012, it was unclear from various media reports whether the case had been settled.

By July, the song had shot to Number 3 on *Billboard*'s Hot 100 and Number 1 on its Rap Songs and R&B/Hip-Hop Songs charts. Deejays (DJs) were calling it the "Song of the Summer."[11] By then, Drake also had a second top ten hit, "Every Girl," which he fronted for the rap group Young Money, put together by Lil Wayne and composed of rappers from his Young Money Entertainment label.

Drake appeared at the BET Awards on June 28, 2009, the day before he was signed to a record label.

A BIDDING WAR

Drake's status as, in the words of a *New York Times* headline, "A Rapper With Celebrity but No Label" was about to end.[14] A fierce bidding war among three major recording labels took place in the summer of 2009. The labels were Warner Music Group, Atlantic Records, and Universal Motown. On June 29, Drake signed with Universal, the same label that put out Lil Wayne's imprint Young Money Entertainment.

Drake and his team negotiated a generous deal with Universal, unheard of for such a new and untried recording artist. He retained all publishing rights to his music and would receive 75 percent of overall sales revenue, as well as earning a $2 million advance. It gave Drake the best of both worlds—keeping his independence while becoming part of a major label.

"Independent is a funny term. I can go independent, but you need distribution, period. You need somebody to distribute your record and you need that army that a label has to really push the record."[15]

—DRAKE, AFTER SIGNING HIS UNIVERSAL CONTRACT

TROUBLE ON TOUR

To promote his rocketing career, Drake went on the Young Money Tour: America's Most Wanted on July 27 with rappers Lil Wayne, Young Jeezy, Soulja Boy, and Jeremih. Four days later, during a concert in Camden, New Jersey, Drake fell on stage while spinning around and seriously injured his knee. "He put his head down because he was in so much pain and then four guys ran out on the stage and had to carry him off," a witness said.[16] Lil Wayne, who had been performing with Drake, tried to make light of the accident. He told the audience he knew Drake's knee was bad, "but I didn't know it was that bad. I thought he was just in a wheelchair on TV."[17]

On September 8, Drake underwent surgery to repair what was a torn ligament. Physical therapy soon had him back on his feet and walking again.

||||||||||||||||||||||||||||||||||||||||||||||||||||||

FIRST EP

Also in September, Drake released a commercial Extended Play (EP) album, which has more songs than a single, but not enough songs to be considered a full-length album. The EP *So Far Gone* contained five songs from the mixtape and two new songs. It debuted at Number 6 on the *Billboard* 200 and sold more than 500,000 copies in the United States, which made it gold certified. To be considered platinum certified, a recording has to sell at least 1 million copies.

Drake performs in New Jersey in June 2009. Upon his return to the state a month later, he sustained a knee injury.

"He's shown the potential to make hit records," said Elliot Wilson, the founder and chief executive of the Web site RapRadar.com. "The kids today want to believe in something. It seems like they want to believe in Drake."[18] With initial success and popularity under his belt, it was time for Drake to make his first studio album.

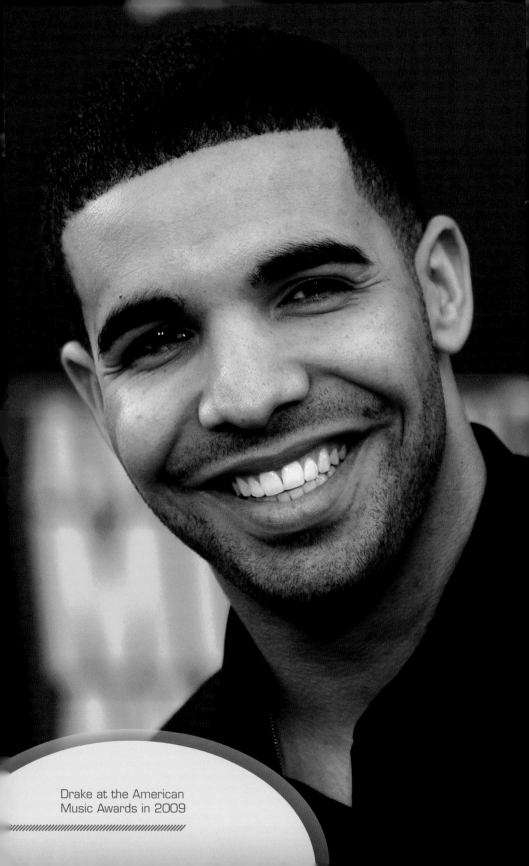

Drake at the American
Music Awards in 2009

CHAPTER 7

Rap Superstar

||||||||||||||||||||||||||||||||||||||||||||||||||||||||||||||||||||||||||||||||||

I n November 2009, Lil Wayne announced to the world that his protégé Drake had completed his first studio album, titled *Thank Me Later*. However, the much-anticipated album, which had already been delayed past an October release, would not appear for another seven months after Lil Wayne's announcement.

It often takes months for a studio to prepare a finished album for release, but the delay on Drake's first album may also have been in part due to the rapper himself. There was speculation of reluctance on Drake's part to go public with his music, fearing it might not live up to the high expectations. "People are so quick to be like, it's not that hot. I know, I *know*, the first day people are gonna hear it and say, oh, that's not as good as *So Far Gone*. No matter what."[1]

Drake soon had the chance to prove—live—that he was a solid talent. In January 2010, he performed at the Grammy Awards in Los Angeles. Drake was also nominated for two Grammy Awards. Both the nominations and the performance were significant, as Drake still had only mixtapes and not official albums out. Although he did not win the Best Rap Song and Best Rap Solo Performance awards he was nominated for, Drake received approval from the crowd and media, as well as some reassurance his upcoming album would please them. Drake was nominated for two additional awards before his album was released. On April 18, 2010, he won two awards from the Juno Awards, the Canadian version of the Grammys. He won New Artist of the Year and Rap Recording of the Year, the latter for the song "So Fly" from his mixtape *So Far Gone*. These

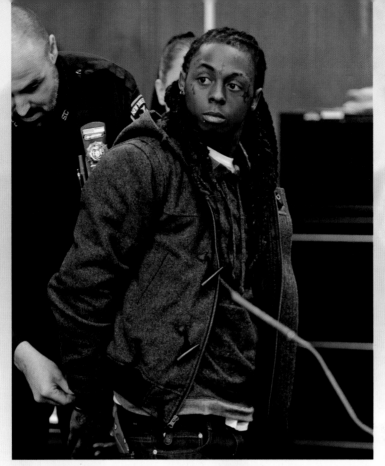

Lil Wayne is handcuffed in court on March 8, 2010, after receiving his sentencing.

nominations and wins were the start of big things to come in Drake's career.

Just as Drake was readying the first single from his upcoming album, he had to say goodbye to his mentor and friend Lil Wayne, who was convicted on a gun possession charge from 2007. On March 8, 2010, Lil Wayne reported to the prison on Rikers Island in New York City for a one-year sentence. He was expected to be out in eight months if he fulfilled the requirements for good behavior and stayed out of trouble behind bars.

Drake deeply missed the man who had helped him achieve his dreams. "I think that for eight months a lot of us will have to work a lot harder to keep hip-hop as exciting as it's been for the last two years," he said.[2]

On March 9, the day after Lil Wayne went to jail, the song "Over" from *Thank Me Later* was released. It quickly rose to Number 14 on *Billboard*'s Hot 100 list. "Over" was an introspective song in which Drake reflected on his sudden rise to fame. Chris Richards of the *Washington Post* opined that Drake questioned his own quick rise to success in the lyrics. The article said the song found Drake "casting a suspicious glance over his own coronation."[3]

||||||||||||||||||||||||||||||||||||||||||||||||||||||||||||

AWAY FROM HOME TOUR

Drake kicked off his first headlining tour, Away From Home, on April 6. The first stop was Pennsylvania, and Drake was excited to get back onstage after focusing more on recording while his injured knee healed.

"I been waiting for this day for a long time. I knew it would be a long time before I got to do my own show. I been training as far as my knee goes, really mentally preparing. I'm super excited. . . . It's gonna be a good night."[4]

—DRAKE ON HIS EXCITEMENT TO KICK OFF HIS TOUR

The night and the tour were successes, with fans singing along and shows selling out. Set to wrap in May, Drake extended the tour through July, adding 35 performances that included international appearances in Denmark, Ireland, England, and his native Canada, among other destinations. While traveling, Drake also opened for rapper Jay-Z for a few performances in the United Kingdom in June.

JAMAICA

On May 5, Drake released a second single from
Thank Me Later, "Find Your Love," coproduced
by producer and fellow rapper Kanye West. By
July, the song rose to Number 5 on the Billboard
charts, making it the biggest-selling single from the
still-unreleased album. West had also produced
Drake's first music video for "Best I Ever Had."
Drake made the video for "Find Your Love" in
Kingston, Jamaica. He worked on the album there
and in Toronto.

The music video tells the tale of Drake's meeting
with a woman who had ties to violent gangs
of Kingston, Jamaica's capital. Drake received
an overwhelming outpour of love from fans in
Jamaica. The Jamaican government, however, was
less impressed. It complained Drake's music video
gave a false and unflattering image of Jamaica as a
violent, gun-obsessed society.

Drake also released a successful third single
from the album. "Miss Me," featuring Lil Wayne,
was released on June 1 and peaked at Number 15.

To promote his album, Drake planned a free concert on June 15, 2010, with the pop band Hanson at the South Street Seaport on the lower end of Manhattan in New York City. The venue was Pier 17, where many musical events are regularly held. But the pier couldn't safely accommodate the more than 25,000 fans who showed up. As the opening act performed, things got out of hand. Fights broke out. Seven people were injured and two were arrested. The concert was canceled. As Drake's bus pulled away, it was pelted with garbage. Drake felt frustrated, as he badly wanted to perform for his fans but couldn't.

THANK ME LATER

On June 15, the long-awaited *Thank Me Later* was released. But Drake was afraid the public would be disappointed by his latest effort.

While the album did incite some criticism, negative comments were in the minority. Most music critics were lavish in their praise. "With penetrating lyricism and arresting melodies, it's a truly captivating debut—a rookie's ticket into the 21st century pop pantheon," wrote *Washington Post* critic Chris Richards.[5] *Thank Me Later* debuted at Number 1 on the R&B/Hip-Hop Albums charts

in the United States and Canada and eventually
sold more than 1 million copies, making it
certified platinum.

IIIIIIIIIIIIIIIIIIIIIIIIIIIIIIIIIIIIIIIIIIIIIIIIIIIIIIIIIIIIII

ROMANCE RUMORS

In November 2010, Barbadian R&B and pop singer
Rihanna released "What's My Name?" a single
featuring Drake. Intense speculation concerning
whether the two were dating had been buzzing
for some time and continued amid the media
during the release. While Drake denied early on
that they had a romantic affair, in a later interview,
he admitted the romance happened and he was
unhappy about it. "She was doing exactly what I've
done to so many women throughout my life, which
is show them quality time, then disappear," he
said. "I was like, 'Wow, this feels terrible.'"[6]

Rihanna, who broke up with singer Chris
Brown over an ugly incident involving domestic
abuse in February 2009, said, "I definitely was
attracted to Drake, but I think it is what it is, like
it was what it was. We didn't want to take it any
further. It was at a really fragile time in my life, so I

Speculation about Rihanna and Drake's relationship rose along with the success of their song collaboration in 2010.

Drake's popularity musically led to other ventures that kept him busy. In 2010, he signed a long-term endorsement deal with Sprite soda as part of their "Spark" campaign. In February 2010, he appeared in his first television commercial for Sprite, which premiered during the Super Bowl broadcast.

In June, the same month Drake made his album debut, it was announced he would make his video game debut in *Gears of War 3*. He was set to play the role of Jace Stratton, a major character in the war game from the comic book series of the same name. Epic Games, the company creating the game, was thrilled to get Drake to play Jace, as was Drake himself. Drake admired the character they had created. Unfortunately, a scheduling conflict prevented Drake from performing in the video game.

just didn't want to get too serious with anything or anyone at that time."[7]

While speculations remained unconfirmed, in a song Drake contributed to in early 2012, the 2 Chainz release "No Lie," he expresses bitterness over how Rihanna treated him, although he never mentions her by name. References to the song "What's My Name?" and to the fame of the woman featured in "No Lie" made it clear to some he was singing about Rihanna. Media attention eventually waned concerning the alleged relationship, and Drake had other focuses, with a new album released and another already on his mind.

|||||||||||

Drake performing in the summer of 2010

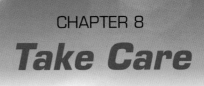

CHAPTER 8

Take Care

||||||||||||||||||||||||||||||||||||||||||||||||||||||

Amid the release of *Thank Me Later* in June 2010, Drake began thinking about making a second studio album. He considered collaborating with Lil Wayne on the entire album. The two discussed this idea during one of Drake's visits to see Lil Wayne while he was in jail.

However, in August, shortly after Drake and Lil Wayne's idea had formed, two other famous rappers announced that they were collaborating on an album. Kanye West and Jay-Z had joined forces, calling themselves the Throne.

|||||||||||||||||||||||||||||||||||||||||||||||||||||||||

RAP FEUD

West and Jay-Z's idea to team up did not sit well with Drake. "I heard some other guys are coming out with an album together," Drake said sarcastically in a radio interview. "I don't know where they got that idea."[1] West and Jay-Z released their anticipated album, *Watch The Throne*, in August 2011. Both Drake and Lil Wayne felt the two rappers had taken their idea. Drake and Lil Wayne decided to abandon their project. "We just agreed that it would be looked upon as . . . It would be sort of this competition," Drake explained. "I feel like it would get caught in this whirlwind of hype."[2]

After the release of West and Jay-Z's album, however, it seemed bitter feelings continued between Drake and West. Media jabs and attacks kept coming and carried over into each man's music. In his 2011 song "Dreams Money Can Buy," Drake made a sly reference to West's $1.7 million

Kanye West and Drake's media feud began infiltrating their music lyrics in 2011.

Mercedes-Benz: "Oh, I never seen the car you claim to drive."[3]

In West's single "Otis," he replied with: "They ain't seen me cause I pulled up in my other Benz/ Last week I was in my other other Benz."[4] Drake's most straightforward challenge to West was his interjection in Lil Wayne's single "I'm On One." "I'm just feeling like the throne is for the taking, watch me take it!"[5]

SUCCESS AND A RETURN TO ACTING

During the time Drake was stewing over the thwarted collaboration with Lil Wayne, his career success continued. He had a hit album, and he performed in a successful string of concerts, including in Europe with Jay-Z, and several sold-out US shows, including one in Philadelphia that sold out within five minutes. *Thank Me Later* was nominated for a Grammy in 2011 for Best Rap Album. Drake also received three more nominations that year: Best New Artist, Best Rap Solo Performance, and Best Rap Performance by a Duo or Group, but he did not win the award for any of these categories. A special behind-the-scenes documentary about him aired on MTV in June, and *GQ* magazine named him their "Man of the Year" in November. The upswings continued that month. Drake's friend and mentor Lil Wayne was released from prison on November 5 after serving 242 days. Drake announced his second studio album, to be titled *Take Care*, 13 days later.

While working on his second album, Drake became anxious to revive his acting career. He had loved being on *Degrassi*, and he wanted to

DRAKE'S DREAM ROLE

There has been significant buzz online that Drake resembles President Barack Obama. Numerous Web sites place photos of Drake alongside those of President Obama to illustrate the striking resemblance. Their looks are so similar that Drake hopes one day to play the forty-fourth president in a movie. He watches the president every time he's on television, studying him as an actor studies a character he will portray. "Nobody's called me about anything, but I just pay attention so when the day comes I'm not scrambling to learn how to speak like him."[6]

Drake has never met President Obama, but he has tried. However, a White House worker said in 2011 arranging a meeting would be difficult because of Drake's Canadian citizenship. When Drake informed her he had dual citizenship in Canada and the United States, because his father is an American citizen, she was more receptive, giving him hope. "I think I might actually get a chance to meet Barack," he said.[7]

move his acting talents to film. However, now an established rapper, it seemed the parts Drake was offered were mostly limited to rapper or basketball player, which was disappointing to him.

In January 2011, Drake was offered a part in the thriller *Arbitrage*, which starred actors Susan Sarandon, Richard Gere, and Tim Roth.

Unfortunately, despite his statement claiming he had time to commit to acting, working on his album led him to withdraw from the film in April. He was replaced by actor Nate Parker. Drake did appear as himself in a cameo role in the sports comedy *Breakaway*, released in September 2011. More recently, he voiced a cartoon character in the animated film *Ice Age: Continental Drift*, released in July 2012, which also featured labelmate and singer Nicki Minaj and comedian Wanda Sykes. Drake also found time to appear in two short films, both released in 2012. *My Name is Syn*, made in Canada, is about a day in the life of a street hustler and his crew. *Grimey*, directed by Drake's friend Al Mukadam, is another crime film about inner-city youth.

|||||||||||||||||||||||||||||||||||||||||||||||||||||||||||||

MORE CONTROVERSY

Drake's music career continued to keep him busy and bring him success in 2011, but he soon was entangled in another musical controversy. In June, he released a single called "Marvin's Room." It was named for the studio where it was recorded, which is also where the late Motown singer

Marvin Gaye had recorded. The song opens with a phone call from a drunken girlfriend, based on a real call Drake received from a girl during a recording session.

> "[In the] Middle of recording I got a call from this girl, and she had been drinking. . . . I just put the phone on the speaker and sat it on the music stand. . . . As I was recording, he [a producer] was taking pieces of the conversation out. . . . At the end of the night we had a song called "Marvin's Room."[8]
>
> —DRAKE DESCRIBING THE "MARVIN'S ROOM" CALL

The voice belonged to Erika Lee, who claimed to have dated Drake. Drake denied the two had a romantic relationship, and he claimed Lee agreed to have the call included on the recording for no fee. Due to her participation, she later claimed she was a cowriter of the song and pressed a lawsuit for royalties. Drake offered her 2 percent of the publishing royalties to end the case. She refused the offer, and Drake came back with 5 percent and a $50,000 settlement. Lee again refused. In a statement, Drake's spokesperson had this to say:

> This claim is entirely without merit and our client has not engaged in any wrongful conduct. . . . Drake tried for months to resolve the matter amicably and he now looks forward to being vindicated in court.[9]

As of June 2012, it was unclear whether the suit had been settled.

||||||||||||||||||||||||||||||||||||||||||||||||||||||||||||||

STRING OF SINGLES

Drake's next focus that year was promoting his upcoming album. As with his earlier album, he first released several single tracks. The first, "Headlines," came out on July 31, 2011, and peaked at Number 13 on the *Billboard* Hot 100. It was Drake's second-biggest charting debut to date. By February 2012, the song had gone platinum in the United States, selling 1 million copies. Drake spoke of how he picks which songs to make singles: "A lot of people pick their single by what's the strongest song. I didn't really do that. I like to make sense that the content is really relevant for right now."[10]

A second single, "Make Me Proud," came out in mid-October. It features fellow singer Minaj. In one week, it soared from Number 97 to Number 9 on the *Billboard* charts. On November 1, Drake released "The Motto," a bonus track from the album featuring Lil Wayne, which debuted on the charts at Number 18.

|||||||||||||||||||||||||||||||||||||||||||||||||||||||

DRAKE ON *SATURDAY NIGHT LIVE* ||||||||||||||||||||||||

On October 15, 2011, Drake was the musical guest on NBC's popular late-night comedy show *Saturday Night Live* (*SNL*). In addition to singing his new song "Make Me Proud," he sang a solo number and performed in several comedy sketches.

In a digital short for the episode, cast member Andy Samberg interviewed Drake in a variety of styles, including "A Matching Sweaters Interview." Drake's individuality shows in his love of sweaters, which are not typically the garb of choice for a rapper. Drake takes the frequent joking about his sweater fondness with good grace and humor. His appearance on *SNL* convinced fans who weren't aware of Drake's acting skills that he was more than a singer.

WORK . . . AND ROMANCE?

Working on "Make Me Proud," the song Drake collaborated on with Minaj, affected more than just Drake's career. The song is about his ideal woman. Drake chose Minaj to be his partner for the duet. Drake claimed to have fallen in love with her when they first met performing on Lil Wayne's Young Money Tour. In August, the two caused a media flutter when they posted comments on the social media Web site Twitter claiming they had gotten married. It turned out the comments were written as a joke, but perhaps the feelings were not. Despite Minaj claiming they are just friends and sometimes-collaborators, Drake appeared to harbor hopes their relationship could be something more in 2010. He said: "I've always really, actually, really had a crush on her, always really loved her, and she's always just looked at me as, like, her little brother."[11] He has also said,

> If there's any woman in my life that's the ideal woman for me, it's definitely Nicki. . . . All jokes aside, Nicki is somebody I could spend my life with because I think we understand each other.[12]

Drake has alluded to having romantic feelings for close friend Nicki Minaj, but the two have never dated publicly.

All of Drake's tracks on his second album seemed personal. He took extreme care in crafting the songs that went into his appropriately titled album *Take Care*. "I knew that I was literally going to take care of making this project and be attentive, be clear, be immersed in it," Drake said of naming the album.[13] He felt he had rushed his first album and that, despite its success, it wasn't as good as it could have been.

> "People loved it [but] I just knew what I was capable of with a little more time. I'm very confident in *Take Care*. I definitely made the exact album that I wanted. . . . I'm very happy with this album. More so than I've ever been with a project."[14]
>
> —*DRAKE ON* TAKE CARE

Take Care showcased Drake's style of reflecting on his life and career through his music. On the opening track, "Over My Dead Body," he addresses his critics head-on, challenging their skepticism that his new album would not be as successful as his earlier efforts. "Lord Knows" is a song created in a very different vein, with a gospel feel and a hard, driving beat. In a song called "HYFR," sung with Lil Wayne, Drake dispenses some of the wisdom he's gained during his career. Other guest artists on the album's 19 tracks include Rihanna, iconic pop singer Stevie Wonder, and the Weekend, a Canadian pop-rock band.

Take Care was scheduled to be released on Drake's twenty-fifth birthday, October 24, 2011. However, clearance for three samples, which are bits of music and lyrics from other artists' recordings that he used on the album, took more time than expected, and the release date was changed to November 15. Drake explained the delay on his Web site. "This music means too much to me to get attached to dates and I do apologize for the delay but I promise that it is only for the benefit of our experience together."[15]

Many fans and critics agreed it was worth the wait. The album became an even bigger success than *Thank Me Later*. It sold more than 630,000 copies in its first week. By May 2012, the album had sold 1.7 million copies. The album was also a finalist for *Billboard's* Music Award for Top 200 Album and Top Rap Album in 2012. On April 1, 2012, the album won Drake his second Juno Award for Rap Recording of the Year. The success of *Take Care* solidified Drake as a serious songwriter and major superstar of rap who was here to stay.

|||||||||||

Drake rings in 2012 on New Year's Eve. The coming year brought him continued musical success.

CHAPTER 9

Living Large

||||||||||||||||||||||||||||||||||||||||||||||||||||||||||||||||||||||||||||

Drake's life had become very different from the life he once knew growing up in a middle-class home in Toronto. He moved into a $9 million mansion in California's San Fernando Valley in January 2012. It had six bedrooms, ten bathrooms, a wine cellar, a backyard tennis court, a pool, waterfalls, and horse stables. His bedroom had a king-size bed that

Besides being an entertainer, Drake is also a businessman. He is a silent partner in an Italian restaurant in New York City. He also designs his own clothes. One piece he designed is an arctic fox fur, gold-hardware bomber jacket worth $5,000. But Drake's dream business venture may surprise some of his fans. "I'm very obsessed with smell so I actually want to—my dream, to be honest with you, is to form a fragrance and lifestyle line like candles, incense, room spray, and fragrance."[2]

required custom sheets. It had a remote-controlled projection system in the ceiling.

Drake's dreams of stardom had seemingly all come true. But not all parts of the dream were ideal for Drake. As he told *GQ* during an interview at his home,

> When I was in my mom's home, I had nowhere to go, no real obligations. . . . I didn't have anything else. And that made for some of the best music, I think. . . . That feeling is hard to capture when you're sitting out here in a space like this.[1]

FAMILY RELATIONS

Drake remained close to his mother, Sandi, and has visited her often in Toronto. She was his date at the Grammy Awards in 2010, where she expressed her pride in Drake. "I've always been proud of my son," she told a reporter at the time, "but to see him come to a pinnacle like this is really quite a journey." Then she added, "He's a great challenge, but in a great way. He is a unique guy."[3]

Drake was growing closer to his father as well. Dennis had nothing but praise for his son's talent when interviewed after the two had dinner at a Beverly Hills steakhouse in April 2012. Both confirmed a rumor that father and son were planning to do a duet recording together in the future.

||||||||||||||||||||||||||||||||||||||||||||||||||||||

LOOKING FORWARD

While there was no third studio album on the immediate horizon for Drake in 2012, he continued to record. He received three Grammy nominations in 2012, including two nominations for Best Rap/Sung Collaboration for "I'm On One"

Drake at the Grammys in 2012, where he was a presenter and was nominated for three awards

with rapper Rick Ross and Lil Wayne and "What's My Name?" with Rihanna. The third nomination was for Best Rap Performance for "Moment 4Life," a song by Minaj on which Drake is featured. Drake did not win any awards that night. Drake also continued to make music videos. In the music video for the song "HYFR," he reenacted his bar mitzvah. The video was shot in a synagogue with actors portraying both his Jewish family members and his father's African-American family. The video then shows a riotous after-party, much like many real bar mitzvahs.

After the video's release, the president of Miami's Temple Israel, where part of the video was shot, disassociated himself and the congregation from it, upset by the bad language used. But then he added, "Jewish youth will see the Drake video at least in part as a reminder to 're-commit' themselves to their Jewish religion."[4]

GIVING BACK

Drake has donated his time, talent, and money to a number of worthy causes. On August 16, 2011, Drake was the recipient of the second Allan Slaight Award, given to a young Canadian celebrity who has been an outstanding philanthropist. Drake donated his $10,000 honorarium to Dixon Hall, which is a community service agency that aids young people in poorer Toronto neighborhoods in achieving their dreams. In August 2012, Drake headlined for the third year at the October's Very Own (OVO) Festival in Toronto. October's Very Own is Drake's media empire that includes his Web site, YouTube Channel, and more. The music festival donates its profits to Jake's House for Autism and the Multiple Sclerosis (MS) Society of Canada. Another favorite charity is Friends of Music Therapy at SickKids Foundation in Canada.

On June 14, 2012, Drake got into an altercation with singer Chris Brown in a New York nightclub. Drake's conflict with Brown, Rihanna's ex who is famous for the shocking domestic abuse he inflicted on her, was alleged to concern Rihanna. Drake and Rihanna recently collaborated on Drake's title song on his album *Take Care*, and they were rumored to have dated shortly after Rihanna broke up with Brown in 2009. Rumors were swirling during the summer of 2012 that Rihanna and Brown had rekindled their controversial relationship. The night of the fight, members of the two singers' entourages threw punches, and it was reported that Brown, his bodyguard, and several others received injuries. It was also reported that Drake and Brown never made physical contact during the scuffle. In August, the company owning the trademark to the club name sued Brown and Drake for $16 million over the incident.

Just as he feels a part of a Jewish tradition, Drake also feels part of hip-hop music tradition. He has seen himself part of that tradition in different ways. The rap culture that emerged in the 1980s and 1990s was based on boastful manhood and rappers that flaunted their power over women, drug use, and violence. Due to younger artists including Drake, this is starting to change. Male rappers can be sensitive and understanding, especially toward women and their relationships with them. "Rap now is just being young and fly and having your [thing] together," he says. "The mood of rap has changed."[5]

||||||||||||||||||||||||||||||||||||||||||||||||||||||||

CLUB PARADISE TOUR

Drake kicked off the Club Paradise Tour in February 2012. He extended this North American tour through the spring and then summer. The third leg of the ambitious tour took Drake to 27 cities in May and June. The tour featured a host of other acts, including 2 Chainz, Meek Mill, J. Cole, and Waka Flocka Flame. For Drake, the tour was not simply a moneymaker but a way to connect with his fans and share a memorable experience. As he put it to one reporter,

> [I]t's definitely not about the check for me. It's about the experience. If the city isn't talking about it, you know, five, six, seven days later, or, you know, if people don't remember it for years to come, then I haven't done my job.[6]

What is in store for Drake in the years to come is yet uncertain. Whether he is still able to find inspiration in his new life of luxury and fame or find the true love he is searching for remains to be seen. How Drake grows and changes as an artist and person will likely continue to be influenced by his underlying self-awareness. This trait and his honest, emotional nature are things millions of his followers hope he never loses. It seems Drake feels the same:

> I wished that we lived in a time and a generation where people would stop viewing my honesty as overly emotional. . . . I want to be remembered as an artist that gave you a piece of me. . . . I don't think people realize that we die, we leave here, and either they forget about you or remember you. And how they remember you is up to you.[7]

‖‖‖‖‖‖‖

Drake performs on his Club
Paradise Tour. He is unsure what
the future holds but aims to remain
true to himself and his fans.

TIMELINE

1986

Aubrey Drake Graham is born in Toronto, Ontario, Canada, on October 24.

1991

Drake's parents divorce and his mother retains custody of her son.

1999

Drake has a bar mitzvah at age 13.

2007

Drake releases his second mixtape, *Comeback Season*, on November 25.

2008

Drake's character is eliminated from *Degrassi*.

2008

Late in the year, rapper Lil Wayne invites Drake to join him on his tour in Houston, Texas.

2001	2002	2006

Drake appears on *Degrassi: The Next Generation* as basketball player Jimmy Brooks.

The *Degrassi* cast earns a Young Artist Award for Best Ensemble in a TV Series (Comedy or Drama) in April.

In February, Drake self-releases his first mixtape on the Internet, *Room for Improvement*.

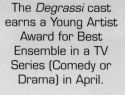

2009	2009	2009

On February 13, Drake releases his third mixtape, *So Far Gone*.

In May, Drake is robbed at gunpoint in a Toronto restaurant.

Drake's song "Best I Ever Had" debuts on iTunes in June and sells 600,000 digital downloads.

TIMELINE

2009

On June 29, Drake signs a recording contract with Universal Motown that includes a $2 million advance.

2010

Drake is nominated for two Grammys and performs at the Grammy Awards in Los Angeles on January 31.

2010

Drake releases "Over," the first single from his first album, on March 9.

2011

On November 15, Drake's second album, *Take Care*, is released.

2012

On April 1, Drake wins his second Rap Recording of the Year Juno Award.

2010

Drake's first
headlining tour,
Away From Home,
kicks off on April 6.

2010

On April 18, Drake
wins two Juno
Awards: New Artist
of the Year and
Rap Recording
of the Year.

2010

Drake's first
album, *Thank Me
Later*, is released
on June 15.

2012

Drake kicks off his
second headlining
tour, the Club
Paradise Tour,
in February. He
extends the tour
into the spring.

2012

In May, Drake again
extends the Club
Paradise Tour for
a summer leg that
runs through June.

GET THE SCOOP

FULL NAME

Aubrey Drake Graham

DATE OF BIRTH

October 24, 1986

PLACE OF BIRTH

Toronto, Ontario, Canada

ALBUMS

Thank Me Later (2010), *Take Care* (2011)

SELECTED TOURS

Away From Home (2010), Club Paradise (2012)

SELECTED FILM AND TELEVISION APPEARANCES

Degrassi: The Next Generation (2001–2009), *Saturday Night Live* (2011), *Breakaway* (2011), *Ice Age: Continental Drift* (voice) (2012), *My Name is Syn* (short film) (2012), *Grimey* (short film) (2012)

SELECTED AWARDS

- Nominated for MTV Video Music Award for Best New Artist (2009) and Best Male Video and Best Hip-Hop Video (2010)

- Won Juno Awards for New Artist of the Year and Rap Recording of the Year (2010, 2012)

- Nominated for Grammy Awards for Best Rap Song and Best Rap Solo Performance (2010), Best New Artist and Best Rap Album (2011), and Best Rap/Sung Collaboration (2012)

PHILANTHROPY

Drake received the second Allan Slaight Award, which recognizes young Canadian celebrities for their philanthropy work, and donated the $10,000 honorarium. Drake has headlined three October's Very Own music festivals, with profits donated to autism and multiple sclerosis foundations.

> "I want to be remembered as an artist that gave you a piece of me. . . . I don't think people realize that we die, we leave here, and either they forget about you or remember you. And how they remember you is up to you."
>
> —DRAKE

GLOSSARY

bar mitzvah—A religious ceremony in which a boy at the age of 13 is admitted as an adult member of the Jewish community.

Billboard—A music chart system used by the music recording industry to measure record popularity or sales.

bootleg—An illegally made and sold music CD or other recording.

chart—A weekly listing of songs or albums in order of popularity or record sales.

collaborate—To work together in order to create or produce a work, such as a song or an album.

debut—A first appearance.

entourage—A group of attendants or associates of an important person.

Grammy Award—One of several awards the National Academy of Recording Arts and Sciences presents each year to honor musical achievement.

hip-hop—A style of popular music associated with US urban culture that features rap spoken against a background of electronic music beats.

mentor—A trusted counselor or guide.

mixtape—Any compilation of songs recorded onto a CD, music file, or other audio format.

paraplegic—A person whose lower limbs are paralyzed due to a spinal injury.

protégé—A person under the care or guidance of someone interested in promoting that person's career.

rap—A style of popular music noted for rhythmic speaking of rhymed couplets set to a strong beat.

record label— A brand or trademark related to the marketing of music videos and recordings.

rhythm and blues—A kind of music that—especially in modern times—typically combines hip-hop, soul, and funk.

royalties—A portion of income from a song or other creative work paid to its creator or performer.

single—An individual song that is distributed on its own over the radio and other mediums.

studio—A room with electronic recording equipment where music, television, or film is recorded.

ADDITIONAL RESOURCES

SELECTED BIBLIOGRAPHY

Caramanica, Jon. "The New Face of Hip-Hop." *New York Times*. New York Times Company, 13 June 2010. Web. 16 Aug. 2012.

Green, Mark Anthony. "The GQ&A: Drake." *GQ*. Condé Nast, 11 Nov. 2011. Web. 16 Aug. 2012.

Hoffman, Claire. "On the Cover: Drake." *GQ*. Condé Nast, Apr. 2012. Web. 16 Aug. 2012.

Lee, Chris. "Drake: From Teen TV Star to Rap Royalty." *Los Angeles Times*. Tribune Broadcasting, 18 July 2009. Web. 16 Aug. 2012.

FURTHER READINGS

Peppas, Lynn. *Drake*. New York: Crabtree Publishing, 2011.

Shapiro, Marc. *Fame: Drake*. Beverly Hills, CA: Bluewater Productions, 2012.

WEB SITES

To learn more about Drake, visit ABDO Publishing Company online at **www.abdopublishing.com**. Web sites about Drake are featured on our Book Links page. These links are routinely monitored and updated to provide the most current information available.

PLACES TO VISIT

The Grammy Museum

800 W. Olympic Boulevard, Los Angeles, CA 90015-1300
213-765-6800
www.grammymuseum.org
The Grammy Museum features exhibits related to many genres of music. Exhibits include a variety of multimedia to create an interactive experience for visitors.

STAPLES Center

1111 S. Figueroa Street, Los Angeles, CA 90015
213-742-7100
staplescenter.com
Drake performed at the Staples Center during his first Grammy Awards in 2010 and received a warm response from the venue's large crowd, which included star musicians. The Staples Center hosts many high-profile events every year, including concerts and awards shows.

SOURCE NOTES

CHAPTER 1. A STAR IS BORN

1. Shaheem Reid. "Eminem Told Drake 'Don't Get Nervous' About Grammy Performance." *MTV*. Viacom International, 1 Feb. 2010. Web. 14 Aug. 2012.

2. Chris Lee. "Words Wrapped in Long Silences." *The Envelope, Los Angeles Times*. Tribune Broadcasting, 1 Feb. 2010. Web. 16 Aug. 2012.

3. Chris Lee. "Drake: From Teen TV Star to Rap Royalty." *Los Angeles Times*. Tribune Broadcasting, 18 July 2009. Web. 16 Aug. 2012.

4. Shaheem Reid. "Drake Didn't Realize at First that He'd Been Nominated for Two Grammys." *MTV*. Viacom International, 3 Dec. 2009. Web. 16 Aug. 2012.

CHAPTER 2. A CANADIAN CHILDHOOD

1. TJ. "Drake Reveals Childhood Struggles: 'I Had to Become a Man Very Quickly.'" *Neon Limelight*. Neon Limelight, 15 July 2009. Web. 16 Aug. 2012.

2. "Drake on His Mother's Influence, Kanye West & Andre 3000, and Obama Being a Fan?" *Vibe*. Intermedia Vibe Holdings,16 Nov. 2011. Web. 16 Aug. 2012.

3. "Drake Biography." *Bio*. A+E Television Networks, n.d. Web. 16 Aug. 2012.

4. Jon Caramanica. "The New Face of Hip-Hop." *New York Times*. New York Times, 13 June 2010. Web. 16 Aug. 2012.

5. Claire Hoffman. "On the Cover: Drake." *GQ*. Condé Nast, Apr. 2012. Web. 16 Aug. 2012.

6. "Drake Biography." *Bio*. A+E Television Networks, n.d. Web. 16 Aug. 2012.

CHAPTER 3. TELEVISION STAR

1. Shanda Deziel. "Drake Superior: The Former 'Degrassi' Actor Is Being Hailed as the Next Hip-Hop Superstar. Is He Also Rihanna's New Man?" *Macleans. ca*. Rogers Communications, 29 June 2009. Web. 16 Aug. 2012.

2. Ibid.

3. "Degrassi TV is Music to Me: Meet an Actor Turned Rapper." *Kayak – Canada's History Magazine for Kids* Dec. 2005. *General OneFile*. Web. 26 July 2012.

4. Chris Lee. "Drake's Prison Correspondence School of Rap." *Los Angeles Times*. Tribune Broadcasting, 24 June 2010. Web. 16 Aug. 2012.

5. Shanda Deziel. "Drake Superior: The Former 'Degrassi' Actor Is Being Hailed as the Next Hip-Hop Superstar. Is He Also Rihanna's New Man?" *Macleans.ca*. Rogers Communications, 29 June 2009. Web. 16 Aug. 2012.

6. "Degrassi TV is Music to Me: Meet an Actor Turned Rapper." *Kayak – Canada's History Magazine for Kids* Dec. 2005. *General OneFile*. Web. 26 July 2012.

CHAPTER 4. MOVING INTO MUSIC

1. Shanda Deziel. "Drake Superior: The Former 'Degrassi' Actor Is Being Hailed as the Next Hip-Hop Superstar. Is He Also Rihanna's New Man?" *Macleans.ca*. Rogers Communications, 29 June 2009. Web. 16 Aug. 2012.

2. Ibid.

3. Amos Barshad. "Drake: The Heeb Interview." *Heeb*. Heeb Media, 18 June 2010. Web. 16 Aug. 2012.

4. Ibid.

5. Shanda Deziel. "Drake Superior: The Former 'Degrassi' Actor Is Being Hailed as the Next Hip-Hop Superstar. Is He Also Rihanna's New Man?" *Macleans. ca*. Rogers Communications, 29 June 2009. Web. 16 Aug. 2012.

6. Marlow Stern. "Drake on 'Take Care,' Rihanna, Chris Brown 'Fight,' Acting, and More." *The Daily Beast*. Newsweek/Daily Beast, 15 Nov. 2011. Web. 16 Aug. 2012.

7. Amos Barshad. "Drake: The Heeb Interview." *Heeb*. Heeb Media, 18 June 2010. Web. 16 Aug. 2012.

CHAPTER 5. LIL WAYNE TOUR

1. "Drake on Lil Wayne." *Interview*. Interview Magazine, n.d. Web. 16 Aug. 2012.

2. Theo Bark. "Rick Ross Says 'I Always Loved MC Hammer'—Say What!" *The Boombox*. AOL, 9 June 2010. 16 Aug. 2012.

3. Ibid.

4. Jon Caramanica. "The New Face of Hip-Hop." *New York Times*. New York Times, 13 June 2010. Web. 16 Aug. 2012.

5. Rob Markman. "Lil Wayne Says Nothing Can 'Touch' Drake's Take Care." *MTV*. Viacom International, 18 Oct. 2011. Web. 16 Aug. 2012.

6. "Drake Talks Young Money, Kanye Comparisons & Ghostwriting." *ComplexMusic*. Complex Media, 29 May 2009. Web. 16 Aug. 2012.

7. Mark Anthony Green. "The GQ&A: Drake." *GQ*. Condé Nast, 11 Nov. 2011. Web. 16 Aug. 2012.

8. Chris Lee. "Drake: From Teen TV Star to Rap Royalty." *Los Angeles Times*. Tribune Broadcasting, 18 July 2009. Web. 16 Aug. 2012.

CHAPTER 6. THE NEXT BIG THING

1. Chris Lee. "Drake: From Teen TV Star to Rap Royalty." *Los Angeles Times*. Tribune Broadcasting, 18 July 2009. Web. 16 Aug. 2012.

2. Jon Caramanica. "A Rapper With Celebrity but No Label." *New York Times*. New York Times, 27 May 2009. Web. 16 Aug. 2012.

3. Carl Chery. "Drake Remembers First Performance at New York's S.O.B.'s." *XXL Mag.com*. Harris Publications, 14 Mar. 2012. Web. 16 Aug. 2012.

4. Jon Caramanica. "A Rapper With Celebrity but No Label." *New York Times*. New York Times, 27 May 2009. Web. 16 Aug. 2012.

5. Jon Caramanica. "The New Face of Hip-Hop." *New York Times*. New York Times, 13 June 2010. Web. 16 Aug. 2012.

6. Shanda Deziel. "Drake Superior: The Former 'Degrassi' Actor Is Being Hailed as the Next Hip-Hop Superstar. Is He Also Rihanna's New Man?" *Macleans.ca*. Rogers Communications, 29 June 2009. Web. 16 Aug. 2012.

7. Ibid.

8. Bruce Pilato. "Hip-Hop Star Has Potent Pedigree." *Daily Variety* 15 June 2010. *General OneFile*. Web. 22 July 2012.

9. Elan Mancini. "Fake Drake CD Sold On iTunes, Rapper Plans to Sue." *XXL Mag.com*. Harris Publications, 5 June 2009. 16 Aug. 2012.

10. "Lawsuit Planned for Fake Drake Album." *Billboard.com*. Rovi Corporation, n.d. Web. 16 Aug. 2012.

11. Chris Lee. "Drake: From Teen TV Star to Rap Royalty." *Los Angeles Times*. Tribune Broadcasting, 18 July 2009. Web. 16 Aug. 2012.

12. "Drake Responds To Kia Shines Claims . . . Kia Backs It Up With Proof." *Hiphopwired.com*. HipHopWired, 18 Sep. 2009. Web. 16 Aug. 2012.

13. Danielle Canada. "DJ Absolut To Sue Over Drake's 'Best I Ever Had.'" *HipHopWired*. Hiphopwired.com, 7 June 2010. Web. 16 Aug. 2012.

14. Jon Caramanica. "A Rapper With Celebrity but No Label." *New York Times*. New York Times, 27 May 2009. Web. 16 Aug. 2012.

15. Shaheem Reid. "Drake Signs With Lil Wayne's Young Money Label." *MTV*. Viacom International, 29 June 2009. Web. 16 Aug. 2012.

16. "Drake Collapses on Stage During Young Money Tour." *AceShowbiz*. AceShowbiz.com, 1 Aug. 2009. Web. 16 Aug. 2012.

17. Ibid.

18. Chris Lee. "Drake: From Teen TV Star to Rap Royalty." *Los Angeles Times*. Tribune Broadcasting, 18 July 2009. Web. 16 Aug. 2012.

CHAPTER 7. RAP SUPERSTAR

1. Amos Barshad. "Drake: The Heeb Interview." *Heeb*. Heeb Media, 18 June 2010. Web. 16 Aug. 2012.

2. Shaheem Reid. "Drake, Birdman Talk About Lil Wayne's Upcoming Jail Time." *MTV*. Viacom International, 8 Feb. 2010. Web. 16 Aug. 2012.

3. Chris Richards. "Drake's New Rap Reality: The Realm of Emotion." *Washington Post*. Washington Post, 15 June 2010. Web. 16 Aug. 2012.

4. Shaheem Reid. "Drake Premieres New Song at Away From Home Tour Kickoff." *MTV*. Viacom International, 6 Apr. 2010. Web. 16 Aug. 2012.

5. Chris Richards. "Drake's New Rap Reality: The Realm of Emotion." *Washington Post*. Washington Post, 15 June 2010. Web. 16 Aug. 2012.

6. Jon Caramanica. "The New Face of Hip-Hop." *New York Times*. New York Times, 13 June 2010. Web. 16 Aug. 2012.

7. Theo Bark. "Rihanna Finally Admits to Dating Drake." *The Boombox*. AOL, 18 Nov. 2010. Web. 16 Aug. 2012.

CHAPTER 8. *TAKE CARE*

1. Rob Markman. "Lil Wayne And Drake to Drop Joint Album." *MTV*. Viacom International, 12 Aug. 2011. Web. 16 Aug. 2012.

2. Shaheem Reid. "Lil Wayne & Drake Scrap Joint LP Because of Jay-Z & Kanye West." *XXL Mag.com*, Harris Publications, 8 Nov. 2011. Web. 16 Aug. 2012.

3. Marc Tracy. "Jewish Rapper's Bickering Beef With Kanye." *Tablet*. Nextbook, 26 July 2011. Web. 16 Aug. 2012.

4. Ibid.

5. Ibid.

6. "Drake Reveals Dream Role to Play Barack Obama In Biopic." *HipHopWired*. Hiphopwired.com, 20 July 2010. 16 Aug. 2012.

7. Marlow Stern. "Drake on 'Take Care,' Rihanna, Chris Brown 'Fight,' Acting, and More." *The Daily Beast*. Newsweek/Daily Beast, 15 Nov. 2011. Web. 16 Aug. 2012.

8. Gerrick D. Kennedy. "Drake: No 'Merit' to 'Marvin's Room' Lawsuit." *Los Angeles Times*. Tribune Broadcasting, 3 Feb. 2012. Web. 16 Aug. 2012.

9. Ibid.

10. Erika Ramirez. "Drake Talks 'Headlines' Single, Says 'Take Care' is His 'Best Project.'" *Billboard.com*. Rovi Corporation, 2 Aug. 2011. 16 Aug. 2012.

11. Mawuse Ziegbe. "Drake, Nicki Minaj Open Up About His 'Crush' On Her." *MTV*. Viacom International, 14 June 2010. Web. 16 Aug. 2012.

12. Marlow Stern. "Drake on 'Take Care,' Rihanna, Chris Brown 'Fight,' Acting, and More." *The Daily Beast*. Newsweek/Daily Beast, 15 Nov. 2011. Web. 16 Aug. 2012.

13. Mark Anthony Green. "The GQ&A: Drake." *GQ*. Condé Nast, 11 Nov. 2011. Web. 16 Aug. 2012.

14. Gerrick D. Kennedy. "Drake Takes Cautious Approach to Stardom." *Los Angeles Times*. Tribune Broadcasting, 8 Nov. 2011. Web. 16 Aug. 2012.

15. Drake. "*Take Care* November 15." *October's Very Own*. n.p., 8 Oct. 2011. Web. 16 Aug. 2012.

CHAPTER 9. LIVING LARGE

1. Claire Hoffman. "On the Cover: Drake." *GQ*. Condé Nast, Apr. 2012. Web. 16 Aug. 2012.

2. Adella Platon. "Drake on Naming Exes in His Songs: 'I Always Talk About Women I Truly Cared For.'" *Vibe*. Intermedia Vibe Holdings, 15 Nov. 2011. Web. 16 Aug. 2012.

3. James Dinh. "Drake And His Mom Share Excitement on Grammy Night." *MTV*. Viacom International, 14 Feb. 2011. Web. 16 Aug. 2012.

4. "Drake's Bar Mitzvah Controversy: Temple Israel President Says Clip 'Not Consistent' with Jewish Reform Congregation (video)." *HuffPost Miami*. HuffingtonPost.com, 13 Apr. 2012. Web. 16 Aug. 2012.

5. Claire Hoffman. "On the Cover: Drake." *GQ*. Condé Nast, Apr. 2012. Web. 16 Aug. 2012.

6. Scott Gargan. "Drake, J. Cole Blaze Through Hartford on Club Paradise Tour." *CTPost.com*. Hearst Communications, 6 June 2012. Web. 16 Aug. 2012.

7. Mark Anthony Green. "The GQ&A: Drake." *GQ*. Condé Nast, 11 Nov. 2011. Web. 16 Aug. 2012.

INDEX

ABOUT THE AUTHOR

Steve Otfinoski is a freelance author. He has written more than 150 books for young adults. Three of his nonfiction books have been named Books for the Teen Age by the New York Public Library. He is also a playwright and novelist. Otfinoski lives in Connecticut with his wife, their daughter, and two dogs.

PHOTO CREDITS

Shutterstock Images, cover, 3, 6, 98 (top); Kevin Winter/Getty Images, 9; Robyn Beck/AFP/Getty Images, 13; iStockphoto/Thinkstock, 14, 96 (top); Charles Sykes/AP Images, 17; Henryk Sadura/iStockphoto, 19; Featureflash/Shutterstock Images, 22; Tammie Arroyo/AP Images, 26, 97; Frederick M. Brown/Getty Images, 31; Peter Kramer/AP Images, 32; Ray Tamarra/Getty Images, 35, 38; Chris Pizzello/Shutterstock Images, 40, 60, 96 (bottom), 100; Jared Milgrim/FilmMagic/Getty Images, 45; George Pimentel/WireImage/Getty Images, 48; Johnny Nunez/WireImage/Getty Images, 51, 59; Maury Phillips/WireImage/Getty Images, 56; Louis Lanzano/AP Images, 63; Matt Sayles/AP Images, 69; John Steel/Shutterstock Images, 72, 98 (bottom); Abdeljalil Bounhar/AP Images, 75; Todd Williamson/WireImage/Getty Images, 83; Bobby Bank/WireImage/Getty Images, 86; Jeff Kravitz/FilmMagic/Getty Images, 90; Shirlaine Forrest/WireImages/Getty Images, 95, 99